THAT'S GROSS!

GROSS THINGS UNDER YOUR FEET

By Greg Roza

Gareth Stevens
Publishing

Please visit our website, www.garethstevens.com. For a free color catalog of all our high-quality books, call toll free 1-800-542-2595 or fax 1-877-542-2596.

Library of Congress Cataloging-in-Publication Data

Roza, Greg
        Gross things under your feet / by Greg Roza.
        p.   cm. – (That's gross!)
Summary: This book describes life forms in the soil and in caves such as worms, bugs, bats, and microorganisms.
Includes bibliographical references and index.
ISBN 978-1-4339-7131-0 (library binding)
ISBN 978-1-4339-7132-7 (pbk.)
ISBN 978-1-4339-7133-4 (6-pack)
1. Soil animals—Juvenile literature   [1. Soil animals]   I. Title   II. Series
                    2013
591.75/7—dc23

First Edition

Published in 2013 by
Gareth Stevens Publishing
111 East 14th Street, Suite 349
New York, NY 10003

Designer: Daniel Hosek
Editor: Therese Shea

Photo credits: Cover, p. 1 (feet) Comstock/Thinkstock.com; cover, p. 1 (worms) Kokhanchikov/Shutterstock.com; pp. 4–5 mashe/Shutterstock.com; p. 6 Michael Pettigrew/Shutterstock.com; p. 7 jy2nic/pond5.com; p. 8 Eric Isselé/Shutterstock.com; pp. 8–9 Visuals Unlimited, Inc./Ken Catania/Getty Images; p. 11 (main image) Visuals Unlimited, Inc./Nigel Cattlin/Getty Images; p. 11 (inset) D. Kucharski & K. Kucharska/Shutterstock.com; p. 12 Joerg Beuge/Shutterstock.com; p. 14 Domen Lombergar/Shutterstock.com; p. 15 Grigory Kubatyan/Shutterstock.com; p. 17 Photodisc/Thinkstock.com; pp. 18, 19 (dust mite) Hemera/Thinkstock.com; p. 19 (main) Photos.com/Thinkstock.com; pp. 20–21 dangerous_disco/Flickr/Getty Images.

Printed in the United States of America

CPSIA compliance information: Batch #CS12GS: For further information contact Gareth Stevens, New York, New York at 1-800-542-2595.

CONTENTS

Don't Forget Your Sneakers! .4

Quit Bugging Me! 6

Burrowing Mammals 8

The Soil Is Alive! 10

Break It Down 12

Creepy Caves 14

Watch Your Step 16

Are Your Floors Clean? .18

What's Under *Your* Feet? 20

Glossary. 22

For More Information 23

Index 24

Words in the glossary appear in **bold** type the first time they are used in the text.

DON'T FORGET YOUR SNEAKERS!

Have you ever walked in the grass with bare feet? It feels great on a warm summer day. However, have you thought about the things you might be stepping on? For example, everyone knows that earthworms live underground. They sometimes come to the surface. Watch your step . . . SQUISH! Now you have worm guts on your feet!

Earthworms aren't the only gross things you can find under your feet. Our world is full of stuff that might make you think twice about going barefoot!

In some areas, there can be more than 1 million earthworms living in an acre of soil!

Gross or Cool?

Worms help mix up soil and make it perfect for growing crops. Worm poop, called castings, contains **nutrients** perfect for plant growth.

QUIT BUGGING ME!

Many types of bugs live underground—ants, beetles, and wasps to name a few. Bugs such as ants and termites live in groups called colonies. There can be thousands or even millions of ants in a single colony, all crawling a few inches beneath your feet!

Have you ever come across a fat, white worm with tiny legs while digging in the dirt? It wasn't a worm. It was a baby bug called a grub! Some grubs are tiny, but others are pretty big.

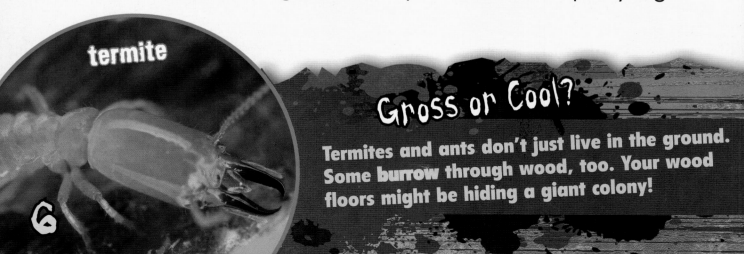

termite

Gross or Cool?

Termites and ants don't just live in the ground. Some **burrow** through wood, too. Your wood floors might be hiding a giant colony!

In some areas of the world, people dig up grubs and eat them—often while they're still alive and wiggling!

9

BURROWING MAMMALS

Many animals make their homes, called burrows, underground. However, not all of them are as cute as rabbits and prairie dogs. Most moles aren't very pretty, but some are totally creepy. The star-nosed mole—with its weird nose and giant digging paws—looks like it came from another planet!

Some burrowing mammals carry **diseases**. Foxes and skunks can spread **rabies** with a single bite. And you probably know why else skunks are gross. They use a gross-smelling liquid to chase enemies away.

Gross or Cool?

Skunks spray a stinky, oily liquid at their enemies. The spray can reach up to 10 feet (3 m) away.

The nose of the star-nosed mole may look gross, but it's for sniffing out yummy bugs, grubs, and worms. It can even smell food underwater!

9

THE SOIL IS ALIVE!

Have you ever picked up a handful of soil? That soil was crawling with billions of microorganisms, creatures too small to see without a microscope. Soil contains **bacteria**, **fungi**, tiny worms called nematodes, eight-legged creatures called mites, and many other life-forms.

These things can be good for the soil and the plants we grow there. However, some microorganisms in the soil can cause diseases in plants, animals, and people. Others may get into underground wells and make drinking water unsafe.

Gross or Cool?

Some nematodes kill bugs by getting inside them. The worms feed on the bug and multiply. Soon, hundreds of thousands of young nematodes crawl out of the dead bug!

nematode seen through a microscope

Nematodes destroyed this potato crop. They fed on the plants' roots so the potatoes couldn't grow.

11

BREAK IT DOWN

Bacteria, fungi, and nematodes are decomposers. They help break down, or decompose, dead plants and animals by eating them. This returns important nutrients to the soil, where they're used by growing plants. Decomposers are the reason things rot. That's pretty gross, but imagine how gross our world would be without decomposers to clean up the mess.

Soil also contains animal feces—that's poop! Feces return nutrients to the soil as well. They provide decomposers with another food source.

Not all fungi are microscopic. Some, such as mold, are easily visible on rotting food.

What is composting?

You can make your own garden soil by composting. It's a great way to recycle and reduce your family's waste. Follow the instructions here:

1. Select a place for your compost bin or pile away from your house—composting stinks! Your compost should touch the ground so decomposers can climb in.

2. Start with a layer of straw, twigs, tree bark, and dead leaves. You can also add dirt.

3. Now add kitchen scraps such as fruits, veggies, coffee grounds, popcorn, tea bags, eggshells, pasta, and peanut shells. You can even add grass, newspaper, cardboard, pet fur, and hair! (Avoid products with **chemicals** and meat products.)

4. Add more dirt and water, and stir.

5. As the days pass, your compost will get grosser and grosser. That means decomposers are doing their job. Throw in more water, soil, and earthworms to speed up the process.

CREEPY CAVES

Some animals, such as bats, love life in underground caves. Other creatures have **adapted** to cave life and can't live outside of them. These animals are called troglobites. Most have poor vision, but their other senses are excellent. Many troglobites are ghostly white or even **translucent**.

Troglobites called olms were once thought to be baby dragons. Their long, slender, white body is translucent, allowing viewers to see the shape of their guts! Newborn olms have eyes, but their eyes lose strength after a few months.

olm

Caves are some of the last unexplored places on Earth. Who knows what else might be lurking down there waiting to be discovered?

Gross or Cool?

A lot of bat guano, or bat poop, piles up in caves. Long ago, people realized that guano could be used for fertilizer. Now

WATCH YOUR STEP

Have you ever stepped on a wad of gum on the sidewalk? It's almost impossible to get it off the soles of your shoes! Thanks to careless litterbugs, you might step on a half-eaten hot dog or a slippery banana peel. Some inconsiderate dog owners fail to clean up dog poop. You might squish a bug or a slug, too.

Think of all the things your sneakers tread on in a single day. Now, imagine what you might be carrying into your home on your sneakers. Yuck!

Gross or Cool?

A study conducted in Japan showed that a single wad of chewed gum lying on the pavement has up to 1 million bacteria per gram (0.04 ounce) of gum!

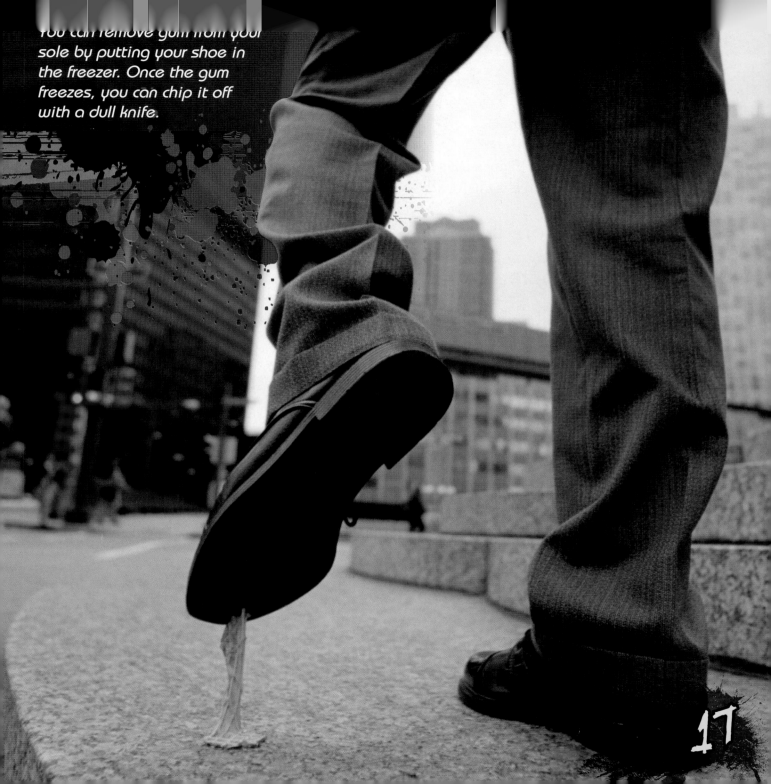

You can remove gum from your sole by putting your shoe in the freezer. Once the gum freezes, you can chip it off with a dull knife.

17

ARE YOUR FLOORS CLEAN?

Most people would like to think the floors in their homes are clean, but are they really? Kitchen and bathroom floors often have hundreds of bacteria per square inch (6.5 sq cm). When you step on those bacteria, you can spread them to other areas of the house.

You might think your vacuum cleaner does a great job, but it doesn't suck up everything. Mold can be a real problem for people with **allergies**. Dust mites eat human skin in rugs and can cause allergy problems, too.

Gross or Cool?

Bleach is the best weapon against microorganisms living on your kitchen and bathroom floors. This strong liquid makes microorganisms fall to pieces!

Hundreds of thousands of kinds of bacteria may be living in your rugs—and dust mites, too!

dust mite

19

WHAT'S UNDER YOUR FEET?

Athlete's foot is a condition that causes the skin between toes and on soles to turn red and feel itchy. It's caused by fungi living in locker rooms, showers, and anywhere people with bare feet spread it. Plantar warts are hard growths on your soles. They grow deep and can be painful. Splinters in your feet can allow bacteria to get in and cause disease.

Now that you know more about what's gross on the ground, you can do more to keep it—and you—clean and safe!

Bacteria and fungi live in sneakers because they love hot, sweaty places. They're the reason why your sneakers start to stink after a while.

21

GLOSSARY

adapt: to change in order to better fit surroundings

allergy: an overreaction by the body (including sneezing and watery eyes) to something that isn't usually harmful, such as pollen or pet hair

bacteria: tiny, single-celled organisms. Many kinds are helpful. Some can cause diseases in humans.

burrow: to make a hole or tunnel by digging. Also, an underground animal home.

chemical: matter that can be mixed with other matter to cause changes

disease: illness

fertilizer: something that makes soil better for growing crops and other plants

fungi: living things that are somewhat like plants, but don't make their own food, have leaves, or have a green color. Fungi include yeast, molds, and mushrooms.

nutrient: something a living thing needs to grow and stay alive

rabies: a potentially deadly disease that affects the central nervous system. It is carried in the spit of some animals, including some raccoons.

translucent: allowing some light to pass through

FOR MORE INFORMATION

Books

Boyer, Crispin. *That's Gross! Icky Facts That Will Test Your Gross-Out Factor.* Washington, DC: National Geographic Children's Books, 2012.

Rosenberg, Pam. *Ack! Icky, Sticky, Gross Stuff Underground.* Mankato, MN: The Child's World, 2007.

Websites

The Dirt on Soil
school.discoveryeducation.com/schooladventures/soil/
Discover more about different kinds of soil and the creatures that live in it.

10 Creatures That Thrive in Caves
www.mnn.com/earth-matters/animals/photos/10-creatures-that-thrive-in-caves
Read and see photos of ten interesting cave creatures.

Worm World
yucky.discovery.com/flash/worm/
Learn more about worms, including how they help get rid of old plants and help new ones grow.

INDEX

ants 6

athlete's foot 20

bacteria 10, 12, 16, 18, 19, 20, 21

bats 14, 15

beetles 6

bleach 18

bugs 6, 9, 10, 16

castings 5

caves 14, 15

chewing gum 16, 17

composting 13

decomposers 12, 13

diseases 8, 10

earthworms 4, 5, 9, 13

feces 12

foxes 8

fungi 10, 12, 20, 21

grubs 6, 7, 9

guano 15

mites 10, 18, 19

mold 12, 18

nematodes 10, 11, 12

olms 14

plantar warts 20

poop 5, 12, 15, 16

prairie dogs 8

rabbits 8

rabies 8

skunks 8

star-nosed mole 8, 9

termites 6

troglobites 14

wasps 6